EMMANUEL JOSEPH

The Uncharted Bloom, Flourishing in Uncertainty with Creativity and Grace

Copyright © 2025 by Emmanuel Joseph

All rights reserved. No part of this publication may be reproduced, stored or transmitted in any form or by any means, electronic, mechanical, photocopying, recording, scanning, or otherwise without written permission from the publisher. It is illegal to copy this book, post it to a website, or distribute it by any other means without permission.

First edition

*This book was professionally typeset on Reedsy.
Find out more at reedsy.com*

Contents

1	Chapter 1: Embracing the Unknown	1
2	Chapter 2: The Courage to Begin	3
3	Chapter 3: Navigating Through Challenges	5
4	Chapter 4: The Power of Perspective	7
5	Chapter 5: The Dance of Adaptation	9
6	Chapter 6: Cultivating Resilience	10
7	Chapter 7: Finding Inspiration in Everyday Moments	12
8	Chapter 8: The Joy of Experimentation	14
9	Chapter 9: Building a Creative Sanctuary	16
10	Chapter 10: The Interplay of Passion and Purpose	17
11	Chapter 11: The Gift of Collaboration	19
12	Chapter 12: Nurturing a Growth Mindset	20
13	Chapter 13: The Art of Reflection	22
14	Chapter 14: Embracing Vulnerability	24
15	Chapter 15: The Magic of Serendipity	26
16	Chapter 16: Celebrating Progress	28
17	Chapter 17: Flourishing with Grace	30

1

Chapter 1: Embracing the Unknown

In the labyrinth of life, the paths shrouded in mystery often lead us to uncharted territories. Rather than fearing the unknown, embracing uncertainty can become a fertile ground for growth. It is within the nebulous fog of unpredictability that the seeds of creativity are often sown. To flourish in the midst of ambiguity, one must cultivate a mindset open to possibilities and resilient against adversities.

Imagine standing at the edge of a vast, unexplored forest. The path ahead is obscured by shadows and dense foliage, and the only certainty is the uncertainty that lies beyond. Yet, it is in this very uncertainty that the potential for discovery and growth resides. Each step forward is an act of courage, a leap of faith into the unknown. Embracing the journey with an open heart and a curious mind allows us to transform the unknown into a canvas for our creativity.

In the face of uncertainty, it is natural to experience fear and hesitation. These emotions are not barriers but signals that we are stepping out of our comfort zones and into new territory. By acknowledging and accepting these feelings, we can harness their energy to propel us forward. It is the willingness to venture into the unknown, despite our fears, that unlocks our creative potential and enables us to flourish.

Moreover, the unknown is a realm of infinite possibilities. It is a space where new ideas, perspectives, and opportunities can emerge. By embracing uncertainty, we open ourselves to the richness of the present moment and the potential for growth that lies within it. It is in this fertile ground that our creativity can take root and bloom, allowing us to navigate the complexities of life with grace and resilience.

2

Chapter 2: The Courage to Begin

Every journey begins with a single step, yet the first step is often the most daunting. Summoning the courage to venture into the unknown requires a leap of faith. It is the willingness to begin that sets the wheels of creativity in motion. By confronting our fears and pushing beyond our comfort zones, we open ourselves to new experiences and opportunities for growth.

Imagine standing at the edge of a vast, unexplored forest. The path ahead is obscured by shadows and dense foliage, and the only certainty is the uncertainty that lies beyond. Yet, it is in this very uncertainty that the potential for discovery and growth resides. Each step forward is an act of courage, a leap of faith into the unknown. Embracing the journey with an open heart and a curious mind allows us to transform the unknown into a canvas for our creativity.

In the face of uncertainty, it is natural to experience fear and hesitation. These emotions are not barriers but signals that we are stepping out of our comfort zones and into new territory. By acknowledging and accepting these feelings, we can harness their energy to propel us forward. It is the willingness to venture into the unknown, despite our fears, that unlocks our creative potential and enables us to flourish.

Moreover, the unknown is a realm of infinite possibilities. It is a space where new ideas, perspectives, and opportunities can emerge. By embracing uncertainty, we open ourselves to the richness of the present moment and the potential for growth that lies within it. It is in this fertile ground that our creativity can take root and bloom, allowing us to navigate the complexities of life with grace and resilience.

3

Chapter 3: Navigating Through Challenges

Challenges are the crucibles that test our resolve and ingenuity. While obstacles may seem like hindrances, they are often the catalysts for innovation. To navigate through challenges with creativity and grace, one must adopt a problem-solving mindset. Viewing setbacks as opportunities for learning and growth empowers us to transform adversity into triumph.

Imagine life as a river, constantly flowing and occasionally encountering obstacles. Just as water finds a way around rocks and other impediments, we too must find ways to navigate through challenges. This requires flexibility, resilience, and a willingness to adapt. By adopting a problem-solving mindset, we can approach challenges with creativity and grace, transforming obstacles into stepping stones.

In the face of adversity, it is important to remain calm and composed. Panicking or becoming overwhelmed can cloud our judgment and hinder our ability to find creative solutions. By maintaining a clear and focused mind, we can assess the situation objectively and identify potential pathways forward. This clarity of thought enables us to navigate challenges with confidence and resilience.

Moreover, challenges provide valuable opportunities for growth and learning. Each obstacle we encounter is a chance to develop new skills, gain insights, and build resilience. By embracing challenges as learning experiences, we can cultivate a growth mindset and continuously improve. It is through this process of overcoming adversity that we can flourish and reach our full creative potential.

4

Chapter 4: The Power of Perspective

Our perception shapes our reality. By shifting our perspective, we can unlock new avenues of creativity and possibility. It is through the lens of optimism and curiosity that we can find beauty and inspiration in the most unexpected places. Embracing a growth mindset allows us to see challenges as stepping stones rather than roadblocks.

Imagine viewing the world through a kaleidoscope, with each turn revealing a new and vibrant pattern. Our perspective is like the lens of a kaleidoscope, capable of transforming the way we see the world. By shifting our perspective, we can uncover new possibilities and opportunities for creativity. It is through this lens of optimism and curiosity that we can find inspiration in the most unexpected places.

In moments of difficulty, it is easy to become fixated on the negative aspects of a situation. However, by consciously choosing to shift our perspective, we can reframe challenges as opportunities for growth. This shift in mindset allows us to approach difficulties with a sense of curiosity and openness, rather than fear and resistance. It is through this positive outlook that we can navigate life's uncertainties with creativity and grace.

Moreover, embracing a growth mindset empowers us to see challenges as stepping stones rather than roadblocks. By viewing setbacks as opportunities for learning and development, we can continuously improve and expand our creative potential. This mindset fosters resilience and adaptability, enabling us to flourish even in the face of adversity. It is through this lens of possibility that we can navigate the complexities of life with grace and creativity.

5

Chapter 5: The Dance of Adaptation

Life is a dynamic dance, ever-changing and unpredictable. To flourish in such a fluid environment, one must master the art of adaptation. Flexibility and resilience are key traits that enable us to pivot gracefully in response to change. By embracing the ebb and flow of life, we can remain agile and open to new opportunities.

Imagine life as a dance, with each moment requiring us to move in harmony with the ever-changing rhythm. Just as a skilled dancer adapts to the music, we too must learn to adapt to the dynamic nature of life. This requires flexibility, resilience, and a willingness to embrace change. By mastering the art of adaptation, we can navigate life's uncertainties with grace and creativity.

In the face of change, it is natural to feel a sense of resistance or discomfort. However, by embracing the inevitability of change, we can learn to flow with it rather than against it. This mindset of acceptance allows us to remain open to new possibilities and opportunities. It is through this flexibility that we can navigate the complexities of life with creativity and grace.

Moreover, resilience is the inner strength that enables us to withstand life's storms. By cultivating resilience, we can bounce back from setbacks and persist in the face of adversity. This quality empowers us to navigate challenges with confidence and determination. It is through this combination of flexibility and resilience that we can flourish in an ever-changing world.

6

Chapter 6: Cultivating Resilience

Resilience is the inner strength that enables us to withstand life's storms. It is the ability to bounce back from setbacks and persist in the face of adversity. Cultivating resilience involves nurturing a positive mindset, practicing self-compassion, and building a support network. With resilience, we can weather any storm and emerge stronger and more creative.

Imagine a sturdy tree swaying in the wind, its roots firmly anchored in the ground. No matter how fierce the storm, the tree stands tall and resilient. Just like the tree, we too must develop deep roots of inner strength to withstand the challenges of life. Resilience is the quality that allows us to bend without breaking and to recover from setbacks with renewed vigor.

One of the key aspects of resilience is maintaining a positive mindset. By focusing on the positive aspects of a situation and finding silver linings, we can shift our perspective and approach challenges with a sense of optimism. This positive outlook empowers us to see opportunities for growth and creativity, even in the face of adversity.

Moreover, practicing self-compassion is essential for cultivating resilience. It involves being kind and understanding towards ourselves, especially during difficult times. By acknowledging our struggles and treating ourselves with compassion, we can build emotional strength and resilience. This self-compassion allows us to navigate challenges with grace and emerge stronger on the other side.

7

Chapter 7: Finding Inspiration in Everyday Moments

Inspiration is all around us, often hidden in the mundane moments of daily life. By cultivating mindfulness and being present, we can uncover the beauty and wonder in the world around us. It is in these moments of stillness that creativity often blooms. Finding inspiration in everyday life allows us to infuse our creative endeavors with authenticity and meaning.

Imagine taking a leisurely walk through a park, noticing the vibrant colors of the flowers, the gentle rustling of the leaves, and the warmth of the sun on your skin. These simple moments of connection with nature can spark a sense of wonder and inspiration. By being fully present and attentive to our surroundings, we can uncover the beauty and creativity that lies within the ordinary.

Mindfulness is the practice of being fully present in the moment, without judgment. By cultivating mindfulness, we can enhance our awareness and appreciation of the world around us. This heightened awareness allows us to find inspiration in the most unexpected places, from the patterns of raindrops on a window to the laughter of children playing in a park.

Furthermore, finding inspiration in everyday moments involves embracing a sense of curiosity and openness. By approaching each day with a beginner's mind, we can see the world through fresh eyes and discover new sources

CHAPTER 7: FINDING INSPIRATION IN EVERYDAY MOMENTS

of creativity. This openness to inspiration allows us to infuse our creative endeavors with authenticity and meaning, enriching our lives in the process.

8

Chapter 8: The Joy of Experimentation

Creativity flourishes in an environment of experimentation and play. Embracing a spirit of curiosity and exploration allows us to push the boundaries of our creativity. By giving ourselves permission to fail and learn from our mistakes, we open the door to innovative ideas and solutions. The joy of experimentation lies in the freedom to explore new possibilities.

Imagine a child playing with a set of building blocks, stacking and rearranging them in endless combinations. This sense of playful experimentation is at the heart of creativity. By approaching our creative endeavors with a sense of curiosity and openness, we can explore new possibilities and push the boundaries of our imagination.

One of the key aspects of experimentation is the willingness to take risks and embrace failure. Each failure is an opportunity for learning and growth, providing valuable insights that can inform our future efforts. By giving ourselves permission to fail, we create a safe space for experimentation and innovation. It is through this process of trial and error that we can uncover new ideas and solutions.

Moreover, the joy of experimentation lies in the freedom to explore without constraints. By removing the pressure to achieve a specific outcome, we can tap into our innate creativity and playfulness. This sense of freedom allows us to approach our creative endeavors with a sense of wonder and excitement,

CHAPTER 8: THE JOY OF EXPERIMENTATION

discovering new possibilities along the way.

9

Chapter 9: Building a Creative Sanctuary

A creative sanctuary is a space, both physical and mental, where our creativity can thrive. It is a place where we feel safe to express ourselves and explore new ideas. Creating a sanctuary involves setting boundaries, eliminating distractions, and fostering an environment that nurtures our creative spirit. In this haven, we can connect with our inner muse and let our creativity flow.

Imagine a cozy corner filled with your favorite books, art supplies, and inspirational quotes. This physical space is a reflection of your creative sanctuary, a place where you can retreat and immerse yourself in the creative process. By creating an environment that nurtures your creativity, you can cultivate a sense of peace and inspiration.

Setting boundaries is an essential aspect of building a creative sanctuary. It involves carving out dedicated time and space for your creative pursuits, free from distractions and interruptions. By setting clear boundaries, you create a sacred space where your creativity can flourish.

Moreover, fostering a mental sanctuary involves nurturing a positive and supportive mindset. It is about creating an inner space where you feel safe to explore new ideas and express yourself authentically. This mental sanctuary allows you to connect with your inner muse and tap into your creative potential, fostering a sense of flow and inspiration.

10

Chapter 10: The Interplay of Passion and Purpose

Passion and purpose are the driving forces behind our creative endeavors. When we align our actions with our passions and sense of purpose, our creativity is infused with energy and direction. It is through this alignment that we find fulfillment and meaning in our creative pursuits. The interplay of passion and purpose propels us towards our highest potential.

Imagine a musician lost in the melody of their favorite song, every note resonating with their soul. This harmony between passion and purpose creates a powerful synergy that fuels our creativity. By identifying what truly excites and motivates us, we can channel our energy into meaningful and fulfilling creative endeavors.

Passion is the spark that ignites our creativity, while purpose provides the direction and focus needed to sustain it. When we align our creative pursuits with our core values and aspirations, we create a sense of purpose that drives us forward. This alignment allows us to tap into a deep well of inspiration and motivation, propelling us towards our highest potential.

Moreover, the interplay of passion and purpose creates a sense of flow, where we become fully immersed in our creative activities. This state of flow allows us to transcend the limitations of time and space, and to connect with our inner muse. It is through this harmonious interplay that we can achieve our most inspired and impactful creative work.

11

Chapter 11: The Gift of Collaboration

Collaboration is a powerful catalyst for creativity. By working with others, we can draw upon diverse perspectives and talents to create something greater than the sum of its parts. Collaboration fosters innovation and inspires us to push the boundaries of our creativity. It is through the exchange of ideas and the synergy of collective effort that we can achieve remarkable outcomes.

Imagine a group of artists coming together to create a mural, each contributing their unique skills and vision. This collaborative effort results in a masterpiece that reflects the diverse perspectives and talents of the group. By working together, we can achieve creative outcomes that would be impossible to achieve alone.

One of the key benefits of collaboration is the ability to draw upon diverse perspectives. Each individual brings their own unique experiences, insights, and ideas to the table, enriching the creative process. This diversity fosters innovation and allows us to explore new possibilities and solutions.

Moreover, collaboration inspires us to push the boundaries of our creativity. By working with others, we are challenged to think outside the box and to stretch our creative limits. This collaborative synergy allows us to achieve creative breakthroughs and to create work that is greater than the sum of its parts.

12

Chapter 12: Nurturing a Growth Mindset

A growth mindset is the belief that our abilities and talents can be developed through effort and perseverance. Nurturing a growth mindset empowers us to embrace challenges, learn from failures, and continuously improve. It is the foundation of lifelong learning and creative growth. With a growth mindset, we can transform setbacks into stepping stones and unlock our full creative potential.

Imagine a gardener tending to a garden, nurturing each plant with care and attention. This process of cultivation allows the plants to grow and flourish. Similarly, nurturing a growth mindset involves cultivating our abilities and talents through effort and perseverance. By embracing challenges and learning from failures, we can continuously improve and expand our creative potential.

One of the key aspects of a growth mindset is the belief that our abilities are not fixed, but can be developed over time. This belief empowers us to approach challenges with a sense of curiosity and openness, rather than fear and resistance. By viewing setbacks as opportunities for learning and growth, we can cultivate resilience and perseverance.

Moreover, a growth mindset fosters a sense of lifelong learning. It is the belief that there is always room for improvement and that we can continuously develop our skills and talents. This mindset allows us to approach our creative endeavors with a sense of curiosity and wonder, and

CHAPTER 12: NURTURING A GROWTH MINDSET

to unlock our full creative potential.

13

Chapter 13: The Art of Reflection

Reflection is a powerful tool for personal and creative growth. By taking the time to pause and reflect, we can gain insights into our experiences, identify patterns, and make intentional choices. Reflection allows us to celebrate our successes, learn from our mistakes, and set goals for the future. It is through this process of introspection that we can refine our creative practice and continue to evolve.

Imagine sitting by a tranquil lake, watching the reflection of the landscape on the water's surface. This stillness allows you to see the world from a different perspective and to gain insights into your surroundings. Similarly, the practice of reflection allows us to gain a deeper understanding of our experiences and to make intentional choices that align with our creative goals.

Reflection involves taking the time to pause and evaluate our experiences. By looking back on our successes and challenges, we can gain valuable insights and identify patterns that inform our future actions. This process of introspection allows us to learn from our mistakes and to make intentional choices that support our growth and development.

Moreover, reflection allows us to celebrate our achievements and to set goals for the future. By acknowledging our successes, we cultivate a sense of gratitude and motivation. This positive reinforcement empowers us to continue pursuing our creative endeavors with passion and purpose. It is through the art of reflection that we can refine our creative practice and

CHAPTER 13: THE ART OF REFLECTION

continue to evolve.

14

Chapter 14: Embracing Vulnerability

Vulnerability is the courage to be authentic and open in our creative expression. It is the willingness to share our true selves, even when it feels uncomfortable or uncertain. Embracing vulnerability allows us to connect with others on a deeper level and create work that resonates with authenticity and emotion. It is through this openness that we can forge meaningful connections and inspire others.

Imagine standing on a stage, your heart pounding, as you prepare to share a deeply personal story. This act of vulnerability requires immense courage, but it also has the power to touch the hearts of those who listen. By embracing vulnerability in our creative endeavors, we open ourselves to genuine connection and emotional resonance.

One of the key aspects of vulnerability is the willingness to be seen and heard, even when it feels uncomfortable or uncertain. This openness allows us to express our true selves and to create work that reflects our authentic experiences and emotions. By embracing vulnerability, we can connect with others on a deeper level and create work that resonates with authenticity and meaning.

Moreover, vulnerability is a source of strength and inspiration. It is through our willingness to share our true selves that we can inspire others and forge meaningful connections. This openness allows us to tap into a deep well of creativity and to create work that has a profound impact on those who

CHAPTER 14: EMBRACING VULNERABILITY

experience it. Embracing vulnerability is a powerful act of courage that allows us to flourish in our creative endeavors.

15

Chapter 15: The Magic of Serendipity

Serendipity is the unexpected discovery of something valuable or delightful. By remaining open to the unknown and embracing the element of surprise, we can invite serendipity into our creative process. It is in these moments of chance that we often find inspiration and new directions for our work. The magic of serendipity lies in its ability to reveal hidden treasures and spark creative breakthroughs.

Imagine wandering through a bustling market, your senses alive with the sights, sounds, and smells of the vibrant environment. Suddenly, you stumble upon a hidden gem—a piece of art that captures your imagination and sparks a new idea. This serendipitous discovery is a reminder of the unexpected moments of inspiration that can arise when we remain open to the unknown.

One of the key aspects of serendipity is the willingness to embrace the element of surprise. By letting go of rigid expectations and remaining open to new possibilities, we create space for unexpected discoveries and creative breakthroughs. This openness allows us to see the world with fresh eyes and to find inspiration in the most unexpected places.

Moreover, serendipity often reveals hidden treasures and new directions for our work. These moments of chance can spark creative breakthroughs and lead us down new paths of exploration. By inviting serendipity into our creative process, we can uncover new sources of inspiration and unlock our full creative potential. The magic of serendipity lies in its ability to

CHAPTER 15: THE MAGIC OF SERENDIPITY

surprise and delight us, and to reveal the hidden gems that lie just beyond our expectations.

16

Chapter 16: Celebrating Progress

Progress, no matter how small, is a cause for celebration. By acknowledging and celebrating our achievements, we cultivate a positive mindset and fuel our motivation. Celebrating progress allows us to recognize the value of our efforts and appreciate the journey of creative growth. It is through this practice of gratitude and recognition that we can sustain our creative momentum.

Imagine reaching the summit of a mountain after a long and challenging climb. The sense of accomplishment and the breathtaking view are a testament to the progress you have made. By taking the time to celebrate our achievements, we can acknowledge the value of our efforts and appreciate the journey of growth.

One of the key aspects of celebrating progress is the practice of gratitude and recognition. By acknowledging and celebrating our achievements, no matter how small, we cultivate a positive mindset and fuel our motivation. This practice of gratitude allows us to appreciate the value of our efforts and to stay focused on our creative goals.

Moreover, celebrating progress allows us to sustain our creative momentum. By recognizing and appreciating the journey of growth, we can stay motivated and inspired to continue pursuing our creative endeavors. This positive reinforcement empowers us to keep moving forward and to achieve our highest potential. Celebrating progress is a powerful practice that allows

CHAPTER 16: CELEBRATING PROGRESS

us to cultivate a sense of fulfillment and joy in our creative journey.

17

Chapter 17: Flourishing with Grace

Grace is the ability to navigate life's challenges with elegance and poise. To flourish with grace, we must embrace both our strengths and vulnerabilities, and approach each experience with an open heart. It is through grace that we can find beauty in imperfection, resilience in adversity, and inspiration in uncertainty. Flourishing with grace is a lifelong journey of growth, creativity, and self-discovery.

Imagine a dancer moving gracefully across the stage, each movement flowing seamlessly into the next. This elegance and poise are a reflection of the dancer's ability to navigate the complexities of the performance with grace. Similarly, flourishing with grace involves navigating life's challenges with a sense of elegance and poise.

One of the key aspects of flourishing with grace is the ability to embrace both our strengths and vulnerabilities. By acknowledging and accepting all aspects of ourselves, we can approach each experience with an open heart and a sense of compassion. This openness allows us to find beauty in imperfection and to navigate challenges with resilience and creativity.

Moreover, flourishing with grace involves finding inspiration in uncertainty. By embracing the unknown and approaching each experience with curiosity and wonder, we can uncover new possibilities and opportunities for growth. This mindset allows us to navigate life's complexities with creativity and grace, and to flourish in the face of adversity. Flourishing with grace is a lifelong journey of growth, creativity, and self-discovery.

"The Uncharted Bloom: Flourishing in Uncertainty with Creativity and Grace":

In a world brimming with unpredictability, "The Uncharted Bloom" serves as a beacon of hope and inspiration. This transformative book delves into the art of flourishing amidst uncertainty, revealing how creativity and grace can guide us through life's most challenging moments.

Through 17 insightful chapters, readers embark on a journey of self-discovery, learning to embrace the unknown with courage, navigate challenges with resilience, and find inspiration in everyday moments. Each chapter is a carefully crafted exploration of themes such as the power of perspective, the joy of experimentation, and the magic of serendipity.

"The Uncharted Bloom" encourages readers to cultivate a growth mindset, build a creative sanctuary, and celebrate progress, no matter how small. It emphasizes the importance of embracing vulnerability and finding beauty in imperfection, empowering readers to connect with their authentic selves and forge meaningful connections with others.

With its blend of practical wisdom and heartfelt storytelling, "The Uncharted Bloom" is a guide to navigating life's complexities with elegance and poise. It is an invitation to flourish with creativity and grace, transforming uncertainty into a canvas for growth and self-expression.

www.ingramcontent.com/pod-product-compliance
Lightning Source LLC
LaVergne TN
LVHW010444070526
838199LV00066B/6177